Sports Fun!

Snowboarding

by Kieran Downs

Blastoff! Beginners are developed by literacy experts and educators to meet the needs of early readers. These engaging informational texts support young children as they begin reading about their world. Through simple language and high frequency words paired with crisp, colorful photos, Blastoff! Beginners launch young readers into the universe of independent reading.

Sight Words in This Book 🔍

a	go	on	the
and	her	or	their
do	into	people	they
down	is	run	this
for	jump	she	to
get	many	some	we

This edition first published in 2024 by Bellwether Media, Inc.

No part of this publication may be reproduced in whole or in part without written permission of the publisher. For information regarding permission, write to Bellwether Media, Inc., Attention: Permissions Department, 6012 Blue Circle Drive, Minnetonka, MN 55343.

Library of Congress Cataloging-in-Publication Data

Names: Downs, Kieran, author.
Title: Snowboarding / by Kieran Downs.
Description: Minneapolis, MN : Bellwether Media, 2024. | Series: Blastoff! beginners. Sports fun! | Includes bibliographical references and index. | Audience: Ages 4-7 | Audience: Grades K-1
Identifiers: LCCN 2023035125 (print) | LCCN 2023035126 (ebook) | ISBN 9798886877694 (library binding) | ISBN 9798886878639 (ebook)
Subjects: LCSH: Snowboarding--Juvenile literature.
Classification: LCC GV857.S57 D (print) | LCC GV857.S57 (ebook) | DDC 796.939--dc23/eng/20230804
LC record available at https://lccn.loc.gov/2023035125
LC ebook record available at https://lccn.loc.gov/2023035126

Text copyright © 2024 by Bellwether Media, Inc. BLASTOFF! BEGINNERS and associated logos are trademarks and/or registered trademarks of Bellwether Media, Inc.

Editor: Christina Leaf   Designer: Gabriel Hilger

Printed in the United States of America, North Mankato, MN.

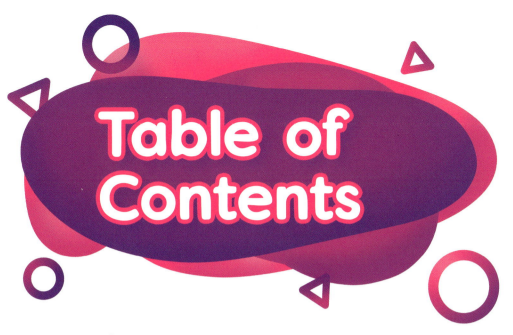

Table of Contents

Ride Time	4
What Is Snowboarding?	6
On the Hill	12
Snowboarding Facts	22
Glossary	23
To Learn More	24
Index	24

Ride Time

We zoom
down the hill.
We love
to snowboard!

What Is Snowboarding?

Snowboarding is a **solo** winter sport. People ride snowboards down hills.

Riders wear boots. Boots lock into snowboards.

boots

Riders wear warm clothes. **Helmets** keep their heads safe.

helmet

On the Hill

Some riders race. They speed down the hill.

Some riders do tricks. They go on jumps or **halfpipes**.

halfpipe

They flip and spin. They get points for tricks.

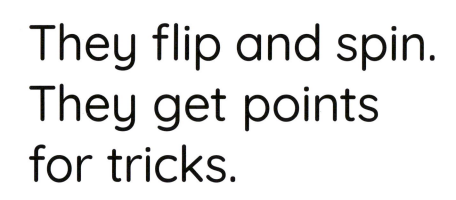

This rider starts a **run**. She lands many tricks.

Her run gets the most points. She wins!

Snowboarding Facts

Snowboarding

helmet
warm clothes
boot
snowboard

Snowboarding Moves

race   flip   spin

Glossary

halfpipes
places that look like a pipe cut in half

helmets
hard coverings riders wear on their heads

run
a full trip down a hill

solo
by yourself

To Learn More

ON THE WEB

FACTSURFER

Factsurfer.com gives you a safe, fun way to find more information.

1. Go to www.factsurfer.com.

2. Enter "snowboarding" into the search box and click 🔍.

3. Select your book cover to see a list of related content.

Index

boots, 8
clothes, 10
flip, 16
halfpipes, 14
helmets, 10
hill, 4, 6, 12
jumps, 14
people, 6
points, 16, 20
race, 12
ride, 6
riders, 8, 10, 12, 14, 18
run, 18, 20
snowboards, 6, 8
solo, 6
spin, 16
tricks, 14, 16, 18
wins, 20
winter, 6

The images in this book are reproduced through the courtesy of: FotograFFF, front cover, p. 1; YanLev Alexey, p. 3; LightField Studios, p. 4; Ahturner, pp. 4-5; Wirestock, pp. 6-7; Hekla, p. 8; Elizaveta Galitckaia, pp. 8-9; PicMy, p. 10; Blue Jean Images/ Alamy, pp. 10-11; GEPA pictures/ Daniel Goetzhaber/ AP Images, pp. 12-13; TSLPhoto, pp. 14, 23 (halfpipes); mjaud, pp. 14-15; Olya Lytvyn, pp. 16-17; PCN Photography/ Alamy, pp. 18-19; Sport In Pictures/ Alamy, pp. 20-21; Sergey Novikov, p. 22 (snowboarding); Maxim Petrichuk, p. 22 (race); AerialVision_it, p. 22 (flip); JulPo, p. 22 (spin); Andrew Angelov, p. 23 (helmets); Drpixel, p. 23 (run); eclipse_images, p. 23 (solo).